What's the Best Little Trivia Book? Volume 3

1,000 Questions About Anything and Everything

David Fickes

Introduction

What you find in most trivia is a lot of erroneous or outdated information or questions that are so simple or esoteric that they aren't interesting. It is difficult to come up with interesting questions that are at the right level of difficulty that a wide variety of people can enjoy them, and they are something that you feel you should know or want to know.

I have tried to ensure that the information is as accurate as possible, and to retain its accuracy, I have also tried to avoid questions whose answers can quickly change with time. Since the simple answer is often not all you want to know, the answers also frequently include additional details to put them in context and provide further information.

There are 1,000 questions about anything and everything. To make it quick and easy to test yourself or others without initially seeing the answers, each page of 25 questions is followed by a page of answers.

If you enjoyed this book and learned a little and would like others to enjoy it also, please put out a review or rating. If you scan the QR code below, it will take you directly to the Amazon review and rating page.

Quiz 1

1) Who is the only person to win two unshared Nobel Prizes?
2) Goldfish are members of what fish family?
3) What was Tom Clancy's first novel?
4) Where is the lowest dry land point in the world?
5) What planet in our solar system has a longer day than its year?
6) What is the only female animal that has antlers?
7) What is the oldest city in the United States?
8) The Emperors Cup is awarded in what sport?
9) For humans, what is the rarest hair and eye color combination?
10) Mount Kosciuszko is the highest mountain on what continent?
11) What is the name for the short, erect tail of a hare, rabbit, or deer?
12) What color is a polar bear's fur?
13) In the human body, what tube connects the kidney to the bladder?
14) What is the captain of a curling team called?
15) What is the heaviest naturally occurring element?
16) What is the only state with the same name as a country?
17) What is coprophagy?
18) What is the more common name of the chaparral cock?
19) What state is the geographic center of the 48 contiguous U.S. states?
20) In 1892, Juan Vucetich was the first person to solve a crime using what?
21) What two U.S. states share the longest border?
22) What university originated the football huddle?
23) What lives in a formicary?
24) What is the oldest national capital city in the Americas?
25) What is the study of fungi called?

Quiz 1 Answers

1) Linus Pauling
2) Carp
3) *The Hunt for Red October*
4) Dead Sea – 1,411 feet below sea level
5) Venus – 243 days for one rotation (1 day), 225 days for one orbit around the sun (1 year)
6) Caribou or reindeer
7) St. Augustine, Florida – 1565
8) Sumo wrestling
9) Red hair and blue eyes - Only about 0.17% of the population has the combination because both red hair and blue eyes are recessive traits where both parents must carry the gene for the child to have it.
10) Australia
11) Scut
12) It has no color; it is transparent and appears white only because it reflects visible light.
13) Ureter
14) Skip
15) Uranium
16) Georgia
17) Eating your own poop - Rats and most rodents have simple digestive systems and eat their own poop to recover additional nutrients.
18) Roadrunner
19) Kansas
20) Fingerprints
21) Texas and Oklahoma – 700 miles
22) Gallaudet University (school for the deaf) in 1892 - They huddled to avoid the other team seeing their sign language.
23) Ants
24) Mexico City – founded in 1521
25) Mycology

Quiz 2

1) What is the highest waterfall in the world?
2) What is the middle day of a non-leap year?
3) Who developed the 1869 Periodic Law that forms the basis for the periodic table?
4) What celestial object gets its name from a Greek word meaning long-haired?
5) What film is based on the Stephen King novella *The Body*?
6) By area, what is the largest landlocked country?
7) The Easter lily is a native plant of what country?
8) In ancient Greece, throwing an apple at someone was a declaration of what?
9) What is unique about the word "eunoia"?
10) What five tastes can a human distinguish?
11) Who was the first NHL player with 500 career goals?
12) What character is the heroine of *The Silence of the Lambs*?
13) What is believed to be the oldest continuously inhabited city in North America?
14) What soft drink first appeared in the Old Corner Drug store in Waco, Texas in 1885?
15) What is the only letter that doesn't appear in any state name?
16) Due to its unique chemical qualities, what natural food can remain in an edible form for centuries?
17) In what country were Arabic numerals first used?
18) What country has the world's longest fence?
19) What city of 5 million or more is closest to the equator?
20) What country has the second-largest Spanish-speaking population?
21) Who is known as the father of history?
22) Who was the only U.S. president to serve in WWI and WWII?
23) What is a group of owls called?
24) What is the only animal born with horns?
25) What is the longest mountain range in Africa?

Quiz 2 Answers

1) Angel Falls, Venezuela – 3,212 feet high
2) July 2
3) Dmitry Mendeleev
4) Comet - from the Greek kometes
5) *Stand by Me*
6) Kazakhstan - the ninth largest country
7) Japan
8) Love
9) It is the shortest English word that contains all five vowels. It means goodwill towards an audience, either perceived or real.
10) Sweet, sour, bitter, salty, umami
11) Maurice Richard - 500th in 1957
12) Clarice Starling
13) Cholula, Mexico - founded in 2000 BC
14) Dr. Pepper
15) Q
16) Honey – Three-thousand-year-old edible honey has been found in tombs.
17) India
18) Australia – The dingo fence completed in 1885 is 3,488 miles long.
19) Singapore - 85 miles north of the equator
20) United States
21) Herodotus
22) Dwight D. Eisenhower
23) Parliament
24) Giraffe - Both male and female giraffes are born with two horn-like structures on their heads called ossicones, which consist of hard cartilage.
25) Atlas Mountains - 1,600 miles through Morocco, Algeria, and Tunisia

Quiz 3

1) Who is generally credited with first saying, "When in doubt tell the truth"?
2) In what century did Michelangelo paint the Sistine Chapel?
3) In *The Jungle Book*, what is the name of the boy?
4) What is the longest river in Asia?
5) What is a baby spider called?
6) What is the process of wave-like muscle contractions that moves food in the digestive tract starting in the esophagus called?
7) What was the number-one U.S. box office film released in the 1980s?
8) What is the westernmost national capital city in North America?
9) Of the 10 tallest mountains in the United States, how many are in Alaska?
10) George Washington, John Adams, and Thomas Jefferson were all avid collectors and players of what game?
11) Who holds the NBA record for the fewest games needed to reach 20,000 points?
12) Hotfoot Teddy was the original name of what American icon?
13) What is arithmomania?
14) What city hosted the first winter Olympics in Asia?
15) What is the point in the moon's orbit that is farthest from the earth called?
16) What was Rembrandt's last name?
17) By area, what is the second-largest country in South America?
18) Who was the heaviest U.S. president?
19) What famous battle took place from July 1 to July 3, 1863?
20) By population, what is the second-largest city in North America?
21) Who is the only person nominated for acting, writing, producing, and directing Oscars for the same film?
22) What is the only Best Picture Oscar winner without any female speaking roles?
23) What is the most populous city north of the Arctic Circle?
24) What is the largest enclosed inland body of water in the world?
25) By area, what is the largest country with no natural rivers?

Quiz 3 Answers

1) Mark Twain
2) 16th century – started in 1509
3) Mowgli
4) Yangtze – 3,915 miles
5) Spiderling
6) Peristalsis
7) *E.T. the Extra-Terrestrial* – 1982
8) Mexico City, Mexico – 99.1 degrees west longitude
9) 10 – Mt. Whitney, the highest peak in the contiguous 48 states, is the 11th highest in the United States.
10) Marbles
11) Wilt Chamberlain – 499 games
12) Smokey the Bear
13) Compulsion to count things – In traditional vampire lore, it is one of the weaknesses of vampires and can be used to defend against them by putting grains of rice or sand out, which they will be compelled to count.
14) Sapporo, Japan – 1972
15) Apogee
16) Van Rijn
17) Argentina – 1,073,518 square miles
18) William Howard Taft – about 340 pounds when he left office
19) Gettysburg
20) New York City
21) Warren Beatty – twice for *Heaven Can Wait* (1978) and *Reds* (1981)
22) *Lawrence of Arabia* – 1962
23) Murmansk, Russia – over 300,000 people at 69 degrees north latitude
24) Caspian Sea – It is considered a lake by some, but it has saltwater and has 3.5 times more water than all the Great Lakes combined, covering 143,244 square miles.
25) Saudi Arabia – 12th largest country

Quiz 4

1) What is the longest-running television variety show in the United States?
2) Silkworms live on a diet of leaves from only what plant?
3) What athlete has the most appearances on the Wheaties box?
4) What is the tallest bird in North America?
5) What is the largest city in the Southern Hemisphere?
6) Who was the last woman to win a calendar year tennis Grand Slam?
7) Who was the first coach with four Super Bowl wins?
8) How many states border California?
9) What is the number of the mobile hospital unit on *M*A*S*H*?
10) What was the first U.S. state to secede from the Union on December 20, 1860?
11) What is the offspring of a cob and a pen?
12) How many players are on the field at one time in a men's lacrosse game?
13) What U.S. state capital is named after a famous German statesman?
14) What country did Abel Tasman discover in 1642?
15) What is enuresis?
16) What fictional detective retired to become a beekeeper?
17) The French village of Domremy was the birthplace of what famous figure of the 15th century?
18) What number on the Richter scale does an earthquake have to reach to be considered major?
19) Frank Lloyd Wright's son John invented what after watching workers move timber?
20) Who wrote the poem "The Road Not Taken"?
21) Morton's toe is what condition?
22) What northern state capital is on the Mississippi River?
23) What U.S. president was shot at twice at point-blank range but survived because both guns misfired?
24) Who is the longest-reigning British monarch?
25) Which state has more of the 100 largest lakes in the United States than any other?

Quiz 4 Answers

1) *Saturday Night Live* – started in 1975
2) Mulberry
3) Michael Jordan
4) Whooping crane – over five feet tall
5) Sao Paulo, Brazil
6) Steffi Graf – 1988
7) Chuck Noll – Pittsburgh Steelers (1975, 1976, 1979,1980)
8) Three – Oregon, Nevada, Arizona
9) 4077
10) South Carolina
11) Swan or cygnet
12) 20
13) Bismarck, North Dakota – after Otto von Bismarck
14) New Zealand
15) Bedwetting
16) Sherlock Holmes
17) Joan of Arc (1412-1431)
18) Seven
19) Lincoln Logs
20) Robert Frost
21) Your second toe is longer than your big toe – It occurs in 10-20% of the population.
22) St. Paul, Minnesota
23) Andrew Jackson – first presidential assassination attempt
24) Queen Elizabeth II – She surpassed her great-great-grandmother Victoria's reign in 2015.
25) Minnesota – It has eight lakes in the top 100: Lake Superior, Lake of the Woods, Red Lake, Rainy Lake, Mille Lacs Lake, Leech Lake, Lake Winnibigoshish, Lake Vermilion.

Quiz 5

1) Which of the Great Lakes do all the others flow into?
2) Who was named Time magazine's Man of the Century in 1999?
3) What classical composer wrote numerous letters and an entire song focused on poop?
4) Who stunned Kentucky to win the NCAA Division I men's basketball championship in one of the greatest tournament upsets ever in 1966?
5) What is the name of Dustin Hoffman's character in *The Graduate*?
6) What European country has the lowest population density?
7) Who is the oldest man to win People magazine's sexiest man alive?
8) The Big Dipper isn't a constellation; what is it?
9) What U.S. state has the lowest highest elevation point?
10) What is the largest desert in South America?
11) Who are the only brothers to receive acting Oscar nominations?
12) In Greek mythology, what did Daedalus construct for Minos?
13) If something is natiform, what does it resemble?
14) If you have caries, what do you have?
15) In the James Bond movies, who is the only actress to play Bond's wife?
16) Who is the principal character in *Fiddler on the Roof*?
17) What food item was invented in a sanitarium in 1894?
18) What U.S. state has the most national parks?
19) The Greek god Apollo accidentally killed his friend Hyacinthus while practicing what sporting event?
20) Who composed *Pomp and Circumstance*?
21) What is the first name of Agatha Christie's character Miss Marple?
22) By area, what is the largest archipelago (chain or group of islands scattered across a body of water)?
23) The human eye can differentiate more shades of what color than any other?
24) Lemurs are native to what island nation?
25) What Soviet leader plotted to kill actor John Wayne and sent two men to pose as FBI agents to assassinate him?

Quiz 5 Answers

1) Lake Ontario
2) Albert Einstein
3) Mozart – No one is sure if it was his odd humor or a mental issue.
4) Texas Western – It was the first all African American lineup to win a national championship.
5) Benjamin Braddock
6) Iceland
7) Sean Connery – 59
8) Asterism - There are 88 official constellations in the night sky; any other grouping of stars that isn't one of the 88 is an asterism. In the Big Dipper's case, it is part of the Ursa Major or Great Bear constellation.
9) Florida – 345 feet
10) Patagonian Desert - 200,000 square miles in Argentina and Chile
11) River and Joaquin Phoenix
12) Labyrinth
13) A butt
14) Tooth decay
15) Diana Rigg – *On Her Majesty's Secret Service*
16) Tevye
17) Kellogg's Corn Flakes
18) California – nine
19) Discus
20) Edward Elgar
21) Jane
22) Malay Archipelago – 25,000 islands making up Indonesia and the Philippines
23) Green – That is why night vision goggles are green.
24) Madagascar
25) Joseph Stalin - He was a big film fan and considered Wayne a threat to the Soviet Union because of his strong anti-communist beliefs.

Quiz 6

1) How many Major League Baseball teams are named for birds?
2) What country or territory has the northernmost national park in the world?
3) Atoms stop moving at what temperature?
4) What book opens with the line "It was the best of times, it was the worst of times"?
5) What language has the most words?
6) Who played Louise in the movie *Thelma and Louise*?
7) An aphyllous plant doesn't have what?
8) What is the scientific study of trees called?
9) What U.S. president has an African national capital city named after him?
10) What breed of dog can't bark?
11) What is the largest snake ever known to have existed?
12) What was the first talking motion picture with the sound in the film?
13) What is the southernmost national capital city in Africa?
14) In darts, what is the highest score possible with three darts?
15) What prehistoric animal from about 150 million years ago is considered the first bird?
16) What is the name for a young female cow that has not had a calf?
17) What actor is in both *The Magnificent Seven* and *The Dirty Dozen* movies?
18) What do frogs have in their mouths that toads don't?
19) What was the first Disney animated film based on the life of a real person?
20) What common spice can be toxic in a dose of two teaspoons or more inducing hallucinations, convulsions, pain, nausea, and paranoia that can last for several days?
21) How many dots are used in each letter in the Braille system?
22) What is the tall, pleated chef's hat called?
23) What country contains the Waterloo battlefield?
24) What common word comes from the Greek meaning "drawing with light"?
25) In the movie *Dances with Wolves*, who plays Stands With A Fist, a white woman who was raised by the Sioux?

Quiz 6 Answers

1) Three – Cardinals, Orioles, Blue Jays
2) Greenland – Northeast Greenland National Park at 76 degrees north latitude is also the largest national park in the world at 375,291 square miles, which is larger than all but 29 countries in the world.
3) Zero degrees Kelvin or absolute zero – equivalent to minus 459.67 degrees Fahrenheit
4) *A Tale of Two Cities*
5) English
6) Susan Sarandon
7) Leaves
8) Dendrology
9) James Monroe – Monrovia, Liberia
10) Basenji
11) Titanoboa – It lived about 60 million years ago and was up to 42 feet long and weighed up to 2,500 pounds.
12) *The Jazz Singer* – 1927
13) Cape Town, South Africa – 33.9 degrees south latitude
14) 180 – 3 triple 20s
15) Archaeopteryx – It was about the size of a common raven and weighed about two pounds.
16) Heifer
17) Charles Bronson
18) Teeth
19) *Pocahontas* – 1995
20) Nutmeg – It comes from the seed of a tropical evergreen.
21) Six
22) Toque – The 100 folds in the toque are said to represent 100 ways to cook an egg.
23) Belgium
24) Photography
25) Mary McDonnell

Quiz 7

1) Who was the first Republican U.S. president?
2) Who is the only MLB player to hit 60 or more home runs in a season three times?
3) What two countries have Sierra Nevada mountains?
4) Alligators are only naturally found in the United States and what other country?
5) What 1979 film has a spaceship named Nostromo?
6) What are baby porcupines called?
7) What is the more common name for serigraphy?
8) In comics, Linda Lee Danvers is whose alter ego?
9) What two animals are on the Australian coat of arms?
10) What U.S state has the largest area of inland water?
11) What explorer brought the first pigs to what is now the United States?
12) What is the name for a female mule?
13) What planet's moons are named after characters created by William Shakespeare and Alexander Pope?
14) How many tusks does a warthog have?
15) What is the smallest population national capital city in the world?
16) Who was the most photographed American of the 19th century?
17) What U.S. president helped to make the word OK popular?
18) Who is the only U.S. president who received a Nobel Peace Prize after leaving office?
19) What is the most densely populated Canadian province?
20) According to legend, what historical figure died of a nosebleed on his wedding night?
21) What is the most populous city in Africa?
22) What is the oldest stroke in competitive swimming?
23) Who was the youngest U.S. first lady ever?
24) What is the westernmost national capital city in Asia?
25) What is the highest mountain in Canada?

Quiz 7 Answers

1) Abraham Lincoln
2) Sammy Sosa – 1998, 1999, 2001
3) United States and Spain
4) China
5) *Alien*
6) Porcupettes
7) Silkscreen printing
8) Supergirl
9) Emu and kangaroo
10) Alaska
11) Hernando de Soto – He brought 13 pigs to Tampa Bay, Florida, in 1539.
12) Molly
13) Uranus – It has 27 moons: Cordelia, Ophelia, Bianca, Cressida, Desdemona, Juliet, Portia, Rosalind, Cupid, Belinda, Perdita, Puck, Mab, Miranda, Ariel, Umbriel, Titania, Oberon, Francisco, Caliban, Stephano, Trinculo, Sycorax, Margaret, Prospero, Setebos, and Ferdinand.
14) Four
15) Ngerulmud, Palau – It has less than 400 residents; Palau is an island nation in the Pacific Ocean.
16) Frederick Douglass – He wanted to ensure a more accurate depiction of black Americans and sat for upwards of 160 portraits.
17) Martin Van Buren – One of his nicknames was "Old Kinderhook" based on the town he was from in New York; during his presidential campaign, people held up signs and chanted OK.
18) Jimmy Carter – 2002
19) Prince Edward Island
20) Attila the Hun
21) Lagos, Nigeria
22) Breaststroke
23) Frances Folsom Cleveland – She was 21 when she married Grover Cleveland in the White House; he was 49.
24) Ankara, Turkey – 32.9 degrees east longitude
25) Mt. Logan – 19,551 feet in the Yukon territory

Quiz 8

1) Who was the first person who wasn't a head of state depicted on a postage stamp anywhere in the world?
2) What individual has won the most Oscar awards?
3) What country has the highest number of museums per capita?
4) What country has the northernmost point in mainland Europe?
5) What U.S. president was arrested for running over a woman with his horse while he was in office?
6) What is the world's third most populous country?
7) What is the largest island in the contiguous 48 U.S. states?
8) How did the duffel bag get its name?
9) What is the southernmost national capital city in Europe?
10) Which U.S. first lady was the first to live to see her son also become president?
11) What country effectively banned Christmas from 1647–1660?
12) What U.S. state has the largest cave system in the world?
13) According to the Bible, how many wise men were there?
14) The character Holden Caulfield appears in what novel?
15) Who has the most career World Series home runs?
16) What is the name for a group of rhinoceroses?
17) What mammal needs the least sleep?
18) What calculation device was invented by William Oughtred in 1662?
19) What are the two categories of harness racing?
20) What is the longest movie to ever win the Best Picture Oscar?
21) What is the deepest river in the United States?
22) In the movie *Night at the Museum*, what is Ben Stiller's character name?
23) What award is the mystery writer's equivalent of an Oscar?
24) What European national capital city is built on 14 islands?
25) Based on the number of weeks at number one on Billboard's Hot 100, who was the top artist of the 1980s?

Quiz 8 Answers

1) Benjamin Franklin - 1847 U.S. stamp
2) Walt Disney – 22 competitive and 4 honorary awards
3) Israel
4) Norway - Cape Nordkinn at 71.1 degrees north latitude
5) Franklin Pierce - The charges were dropped due to a lack of evidence.
6) United States
7) Long Island
8) Duffel, Belgium – The thick cloth used to make the bag originated there.
9) Valletta, Malta - 35.9 degrees north latitude
10) Barbara Bush
11) England - Puritans believed that people needed strict rules to be religious and that any kind of merrymaking was sinful.
12) Kentucky - Mammoth Cave, located near Brownsville, Kentucky, is the longest cave in the world, measuring 405 miles.
13) It doesn't say. It says wise men and mentions the gifts; there is no indication of how many wise men.
14) Catcher in the Rye
15) Mickey Mantle - 18
16) Crash
17) Giraffes – On average, they only sleep 30 minutes a day, just a few minutes at a time.
18) Slide rule
19) Trotting and pacing
20) *Gone with the Wind* - 238 minutes
21) St. Lawrence River - 250 feet maximum depth, 8th deepest in the world
22) Larry Daley
23) Edgar – after Edgar Allan Poe
24) Stockholm, Sweden
25) Michael Jackson

Quiz 9

1) What is the longest-running U.S. scripted primetime television show of all time?

2) What is the highest elevation U.S. state capital?

3) In 1958, a B-47 carrying an atomic bomb larger than the one dropped on Nagasaki accidentally dropped it on what U.S. state?

4) What bird has the biggest brain relative to its body size?

5) What do astronomers call a giant cloud of gas and dust?

6) What is the only creature that can turn its stomach inside out?

7) What is the least populous U.S. state capital?

8) What was Walt Disney's first animated feature film?

9) What are the Magellanic Clouds?

10) Who in literature is told to "Begin at the beginning and go on till you come to the end; then stop"?

11) What is the only insect that has both a king and a queen?

12) What two birds can swim but not fly?

13) A newborn Bactrian camel has how many humps?

14) What U.S. president was reportedly involved in over 100 duels?

15) What outdoor game is won by "pegging out"?

16) Who was the oldest person to sign the Declaration of Independence?

17) By area, what is the largest country with English as an official language?

18) What famous priest ministered to the Molokai lepers from 1873 until his death?

19) What fibrous protein is the main constituent of hair and nails?

20) What island country has the Bahamas to the north and Jamaica to the south?

21) The movie *The Greatest Game Ever Played*, starring Shia LaBeouf, is based on a true story about what major sports championship?

22) By area, what is the largest country entirely within the Southern Hemisphere?

23) What U.S. state is named after an English county?

24) What is the most populous national capital city in the world?

25) What is the point in the orbit of the moon or a satellite when it is nearest the earth called?

Quiz 9 Answers

1) *The Simpsons* – started in 1989
2) Santa Fe, New Mexico – 7,000 feet
3) South Carolina - The core of the bomb was still on the plane, so there wasn't a nuclear explosion, but the 6,000 pounds of conventional high explosives detonated. The bomb fell on a garden in a rural area and created a 35-foot-deep by 75-foot-wide crater and destroyed the nearby house and outbuildings. Fortunately, no one was killed, and there were only minor injuries.
4) Hummingbird – over 4% of its body weight
5) Nebula
6) Starfish
7) Montpelier, Vermont
8) *Snow White and the Seven Dwarfs* – 1937
9) Galaxies
10) Alice - *Alice's Adventures in Wonderland*
11) Termite - The king helps found the colony with the queen and will mate with the queen during his life. There may be more than one pair of kings and queens in the termite mound.
12) Penguin and flightless cormorant
13) Zero - Baby camels don't get their humps until they start eating solid food.
14) Andrew Jackson
15) Croquet
16) Benjamin Franklin – age 70 at the time
17) Canada
18) Father Damien
19) Keratin
20) Cuba
21) U.S. Open – golf
22) Australia – Brazil is larger, but a small portion of Brazil is in the Northern Hemisphere.
23) New Hampshire
24) Beijing, China
25) Perigee

Quiz 10

1) What was the last Rogers and Hammerstein musical?
2) Based on participants, soccer is the most popular sport in the world; what is the second most popular sport?
3) By area, Vatican City is the world's smallest country; what is the second smallest?
4) Who wrote *La Traviata*?
5) What two U.S. states have a lowest elevation point below sea level?
6) What country has the northernmost point in Africa?
7) Who has the most acting Oscar nominations?
8) Who was Don Quixote's sidekick?
9) What is the hottest planet in our solar system?
10) In what film did Paul Newman's character eat 50 hard-boiled eggs?
11) What country is the largest mango producer in the world?
12) What is the only country to lie completely above 1,000 meters elevation?
13) What is the oldest national capital city in the world?
14) By area, what is the largest lake entirely within one U.S. state?
15) What is the name for a male alligator?
16) Which of the basic tastes can't cats taste?
17) What is the most densely populated European country?
18) What U.S. state has the longest border with Canada?
19) Who was the first female U.S. Attorney General?
20) John Henry Deutchendorf became famous under what name?
21) What land animal can go the longest without drinking water?
22) What natural landmark was the inspiration for the song "America the Beautiful"?
23) What is the most populous national capital city in South America?
24) By land area, what was the largest empire in world history?
25) How old is Juliet in Shakespeare's *Romeo and Juliet*?

Quiz 10 Answers

1) *The Sound of Music*
2) Badminton – followed by field hockey
3) Monaco – 0.78 square miles
4) Giuseppe Verdi
5) California and Louisiana
6) Tunisia - Iles des Chiens at 37.5 degrees north latitude
7) Meryl Streep
8) Sancho Panza
9) Venus – 864 degrees Fahrenheit
10) *Cool Hand Luke* - 1967
11) India
12) Lesotho
13) Damascus, Syria - inhabited for about 11,000 years
14) Great Salt Lake – 1,699 square miles
15) Bull
16) Sweet – They don't have taste receptors for sweet; this applies to all cats, domestic and wild.
17) Monaco
18) Alaska
19) Janet Reno - 1993
20) John Denver
21) Kangaroo rat - They can go their whole life of 3-5 years without drinking.
22) Pikes Peak
23) Lima, Peru
24) British Empire - In 1922, it ruled over about 24% of the world's land.
25) 13

Quiz 11

1) Located near the root of human hair follicles, the arrector pili muscles are responsible for what phenomenon?
2) In *The Canterbury Tales*, what were the pilgrims traveling to visit?
3) What did Marie Curie name the first element she discovered?
4) What continent has the largest number of Roman Catholics?
5) In humans, which ear is better at receiving sounds from speech?
6) What is the capital of the Canadian province of Saskatchewan?
7) What is the most abundant wild bird species?
8) What country has three capital cities?
9) What country has the westernmost point in North America?
10) After the Himalayas, what is the second-highest mountain range in the world?
11) What was the first bird domesticated by man?
12) What Jane Austen novel was originally titled *First Impressions*?
13) Rounded to the nearest 100 years, how long before Christopher Columbus did Leif Erikson arrive in North America?
14) What is the name for a group of locusts?
15) What is the second-largest wine-producing U.S. state?
16) What news organization has won the most Pulitzer Prizes?
17) Where are a cricket's ears located?
18) How did the name Muppet originate for the characters on *The Muppet Show*?
19) What planet in our solar system has the most moons?
20) What is the most populous city in Canada?
21) What is the only major city located on two continents?
22) What male actor has the most acting Oscar nominations?
23) What is the name of the dog on the Cracker Jack box?
24) What is the world's oldest tennis tournament?
25) According to the Bible, what are Adam and Eve's three named children?

Quiz 11 Answers

1) Goosebumps
2) Thomas Becket's tomb
3) Polonium - after her native country of Poland
4) South America
5) Right ear - The left ear is more sensitive to the sounds of music.
6) Regina
7) Red-billed quelea – They are sparrow-sized birds found in sub-Saharan Africa; their population is estimated at 1.5 billion.
8) South Africa - Pretoria is the administrative capital; Cape Town is the legislative capital, and Bloemfontein is the judicial capital.
9) United States - Amatignak Island, Alaska at 179.2 degrees west longitude
10) Karakoram Range - Pakistan, China, India
11) Goose
12) *Pride and Prejudice*
13) 500 years - Erikson arrived in Newfoundland in about 1000 AD.
14) Plague
15) Washington
16) New York Times
17) Front legs
18) It is a combination of the words marionette and puppet.
19) Jupiter – 63
20) Toronto
21) Istanbul, Turkey
22) Jack Nicholson
23) Bingo
24) Wimbledon - 1877
25) Cain, Abel, Seth

Quiz 12

1) What is the only Dutch-speaking country in South America?
2) The greatest distance between any two U.S. states is between which two states?
3) What is extracted from the ore cinnabar?
4) Who was the first U.S. president with facial hair?
5) What U.S. state was named after the future King James II of England?
6) The term ursine relates to what kind of animals?
7) Why is a giraffe's tongue black or purple?
8) What current multi-organ animal has existed the longest?
9) What is the most common first name of U.S. presidents?
10) What nationality was the first person in space who wasn't American or Russian?
11) The United States has more airports than any other country; what country has the second most?
12) What is the only tree that grows in saltwater?
13) What horse has the fastest times ever for the Kentucky Derby, Preakness, and Belmont?
14) Who was the first novelist to present a typed manuscript to their publisher?
15) What did Lucien B. Smith invent in 1867 that had a great impact on the American west?
16) What country has the oldest city in Europe?
17) What U.S. television series had 25 different actors fill the six regular roles on the show over its run?
18) By area, what is the largest bay in the world?
19) In the movie, what actor led *The Dirty Dozen*?
20) In golf, what do you call a score of four under par on a single hole?
21) What American novel was the first to sell 1 million copies?
22) What is the only continent with land in all four hemispheres?
23) Who plays Susan Walker, the little girl who doesn't believe in Santa Claus, in the movie *Miracle on 34th Street*?
24) What is the only U.S. state capital without a McDonald's?
25) What is the only animal in the world with cube-shaped poop?

Quiz 12 Answers

1) Suriname – former Dutch colony
2) Hawaii and Florida – 5,859 miles from Log Point, Elliot Key, Florida, and Kure Island, Hawaii
3) Mercury
4) John Quincy Adams
5) New York – He was the Duke of York.
6) Bears
7) To prevent sunburn – It is exposed a lot of the time while they eat.
8) Jellyfish – They evolved 550 million years ago and have no brain or nervous system, and their body is 90% water.
9) James – six presidents
10) Czech – Vladimir Remek in 1978
11) Brazil – about one-third as many as the United States
12) Mangrove
13) Secretariat
14) Mark Twain
15) Barbed wire
16) Bulgaria – The city of Plovdiv was founded about 6000 BC.
17) *Law & Order* (1990–2010)
18) Bay of Bengal – 839,000 square miles
19) Lee Marvin
20) Condor – There have only been four verified; all were hole-in-ones on par-five holes.
21) *Uncle Tom's Cabin* – published in 1852
22) Africa
23) Natalie Wood
24) Montpelier, Vermont
25) Wombat – It appears to be due to the irregular shape and elasticity of their intestines.

Quiz 13

1) How many states are needed to ratify an amendment to the U.S. Constitution?
2) What is the deepest river in Europe?
3) What is the Statue of Liberty made of?
4) In the movie, who did Babe the pig work for?
5) What MLB pitcher has the career record for most wins?
6) The character Marion Crane died famously in what film?
7) What state has the lowest elevation land point in the United States?
8) In Greek mythology, who was the youngest son of Cronos and Rhea?
9) What was the first city to reach a population of 1 million people?
10) What is the only human organ that can float in water?
11) What was the first film to win at least 10 Oscars?
12) What is the largest cocoa-producing country?
13) How many horses are there on a polo team?
14) Who was the first U.S. president born outside the contiguous 48 states?
15) What was Mahatma Gandhi's profession?
16) What is the only film where cartoon characters from Walt Disney and Warner Brothers appear together?
17) What is the word for the day after tomorrow?
18) Who was disqualified for performance-enhancing drugs after winning the men's 100 meters at the 1988 Olympic games?
19) What was the last country to host both the summer and the winter Olympics in the same year?
20) What are the tufts of hair in a cat's ear called?
21) What fictional doctor is the main character in a series of books by Hugh Lofting?
22) What animal has the highest blood pressure?
23) Who originated the quantum theory and won the 1918 Nobel Prize in Physics for his work?
24) What animal gives birth to the largest young?
25) How many colored dots are on a Twister game mat?

Quiz 13 Answers

1) 38 – 75% of the states
2) Danube - 584 feet maximum depth, 3rd deepest in the world
3) Copper - About 62,000 pounds of copper were used to create it, and it looked like a new penny when it was first created.
4) Farmer Hoggett
5) Cy Young – 511 wins
6) *Psycho* (1960) – shower scene
7) California - Death Valley at 279 feet below sea level
8) Zeus
9) Rome – 5 BC
10) Lungs - They contain about 300 million balloon-like structures called alveoli that replace the carbon dioxide waste in your blood with oxygen.
11) *Ben-Hur* (1959)
12) Ivory Coast (Cote d'Ivoire)
13) Four
14) Barack Obama
15) Lawyer
16) *Who Framed Roger Rabbit* – 1988
17) Overmorrow
18) Ben Johnson
19) Germany – 1936
20) Ear furnishings - They help keep out dirt, direct sounds, and insulate the ears.
21) Doctor Dolittle
22) Giraffe – about 300 over 200
23) Max Planck
24) Blue whale – Calves are about 23 feet long and weigh 5,000 to 6,000 pounds.
25) 24

Quiz 14

1) By area, what is the largest Mediterranean island?
2) In the Tolkien novels, what is the name of Gandalf's horse?
3) What two families have three generations of Oscar winners?
4) What U.S. Constitutional amendment ended slavery?
5) Who was the only U.S. president who made his own clothes?
6) What is the least densely populated Asian country?
7) What country's flag has the most stars?
8) In humans, which lung (right or left) is always larger?
9) What is the largest cell in the human body?
10) What is the driest continent?
11) What was the number-one U.S. box office film released in the 1970s?
12) What is the only continent without glaciers?
13) What was the only U.S. soil Japan occupied during WWII?
14) What is the name of the chemical process used to harden rubber by treating it with sulfur?
15) What is the world's largest rodent?
16) Including fast food, what is the oldest restaurant chain in the United States?
17) Who took dictation from Perry Mason?
18) What are the small strips of wood, plastic, or metal between individual panes of glass called?
19) What element is named after the seventh planet from the sun?
20) What U.S. president worked as a lifeguard?
21) What was Shakespeare's last completed play?
22) What insect did Napoleon use as his official emblem?
23) What is the only G-rated movie to win the Best Picture Oscar?
24) What is the rarest hair color in the world?
25) What Is the most popular street name in the United States?

Quiz 14 Answers

1) Sicily – 9,927 square miles
2) Shadowfax
3) Huston (Walter, John, and Anjelica) and Coppola (Carmine, Francis Ford, and Sofia)
4) 13th
5) Andrew Johnson – He had been a tailor's apprentice and opened a tailor shop; he made his own clothes most of his life.
6) Mongolia
7) United States
8) Right - The left lung is smaller to leave enough room for your heart.
9) Female egg
10) Antarctica – about eight inches of precipitation annually
11) *Star Wars* – 1977
12) Australia
13) Aleutian Islands – two remote islands
14) Vulcanization - invented by Charles Goodyear
15) Capybara – up to 150 pounds
16) A&W – founded in Lodi, California, in 1919
17) Della Street
18) Muntins
19) Uranium
20) Ronald Reagan
21) *The Tempest*
22) Honeybee
23) *Oliver!* - 1968
24) Red - less than 2% of the population
25) Park

Quiz 15

1) In what month did the Russian October Revolution take place?
2) Where on the human body is the thinnest skin?
3) What two elements make up most of the earth's core?
4) What ocean has about 75% of the world's volcanoes?
5) What is the name of the process where a solid turns directly into a gas without passing through the liquid phase?
6) What is the least visited country in the world?
7) What is the only known animal to regularly prey on adult bears?
8) What was the first story to feature Sherlock Holmes?
9) By area, what is the largest country in the Southern Hemisphere?
10) What U.S. president is commonly credited with inventing the swivel chair?
11) What country has the oldest mountain range in the world?
12) What animal has more neck vertebrae than any other warm-blooded animal?
13) What woman has won the most Oscars?
14) What English word has the most definitions?
15) Who was the last man to win a calendar year tennis Grand Slam?
16) What toy was originally called the Pluto Platter?
17) What U.S. president's wife saw him elected but died before his inauguration?
18) What do Indianapolis 500 winners traditionally drink in the winner's circle?
19) What kind of animal are the Canary Islands named after?
20) What is the only continent without a major desert?
21) By land area, what is the largest U.S. state capital city?
22) What is the largest marsupial?
23) Barbara Gordon is better known as what comic book alter ego?
24) What country has the world's longest freshwater beach?
25) How many provinces does Canada have?

Quiz 15 Answers

1) November - It was October in the old Julian calendar.
2) Eyelid (0.05 mm thick) – The palms and soles of the feet are the thickest at 1.5 mm.
3) Iron and nickel
4) Pacific
5) Sublimation
6) Tuvalu - It is the fourth-smallest country in the world with 10 square miles across nine islands in the Pacific midway between Hawaii and Australia. It has about 2,000 visitors annually.
7) Tiger
8) *A Study in Scarlet*
9) Brazil – A small portion is in the Northern Hemisphere.
10) Thomas Jefferson
11) South Africa - The Barberton Greenstone Belt is 3.5 billion years old with a maximum elevation of 5,900 feet.
12) Swan - 24 vertebrae
13) Edith Head – eight for costume design
14) Set – 464 definitions in the Oxford English dictionary
15) Rod Laver - 1969
16) Frisbee
17) Andrew Jackson
18) Milk
19) Dogs – The name comes from the Latin "canaria" for dog; when the first Europeans arrived, they found large dogs on Gran Canaria.
20) Europe
21) Juneau, Alaska - 2,717 square miles
22) Red kangaroo - It is up to 5.3 feet from its head to rump, and its tail can be up to 3.6 feet long. It weighs about 200 pounds.
23) Batgirl
24) Canada – Wasaga Beach on the shores of Lake Huron is 14 miles long.
25) 10 – Alberta, British Columbia, Manitoba, New Brunswick, Newfoundland and Labrador, Nova Scotia, Ontario, Prince Edward Island, Quebec, Saskatchewan

Quiz 16

1) In cricket, how many runs are scored if the ball is hit over the boundary without bouncing?
2) If cats are feline, what are sheep?
3) What is the only music group to play on all seven continents?
4) What book contains the line "It is a truth universally acknowledged that a single man in possession of a good fortune must be in want of a wife"?
5) What is the loudest land animal?
6) The Statue of Liberty stands on what island?
7) What is the southern version of the aurora borealis (northern lights) called?
8) In what country was Greenpeace founded in 1971?
9) What was the last province to become part of Canada?
10) How many stars were on the U.S flag in 1913?
11) According to Ernest Hemmingway, a man must plant a tree, fight a bull, have a son, and what other thing to be a man?
12) What Best Picture Oscar-winning film has the longest title?
13) What is the name for the point in a planet's orbit when it is nearest the sun?
14) Who was the first honorary U.S. citizen?
15) What river has the largest drainage basin area in the world?
16) What was the name of the apostle who replaced Judas Iscariot?
17) What is the highest waterfall in the United States?
18) What is the world's most populous large (20 pounds or more average) mammal?
19) What science deals with the structure of the universe and its origin?
20) What creature can be Indian, White, or Broad Lipped?
21) What is the easternmost U.S. state capital?
22) What is the piece of cardboard that goes around your hot cup of coffee called?
23) Kim Campbell was the first female prime minister of what country?
24) Who is the oldest living artist to have a song on Billboard's Hot 100?
25) On the human body, what is the niddick?

Quiz 16 Answers

1) Six
2) Ovine
3) Metallica
4) *Pride and Prejudice*
5) Howler monkey – Their howls can be up to 140 decibels and can be heard 3 miles away.
6) Liberty Island
7) Aurora australis
8) Canada
9) Newfoundland and Labrador – 1949
10) 48 – Alaska and Hawaii weren't states yet.
11) Write a book
12) *The Lord of the Rings: The Return of the King* – 2003
13) Perihelion
14) Winston Churchill
15) Amazon – 2.7 million square miles drainage basin
16) Matthias
17) Yosemite Falls – 2,425 feet
18) Humans
19) Cosmology
20) Rhinoceros
21) Augusta, Maine
22) Zarf
23) Canada – June 25 to November 4, 1993
24) Tony Bennet – age 85 in 2011
25) Nape of the neck

Quiz 17

1) If a giraffe has seven neck vertebrae, how many does a mouse have?
2) What is the flattest U.S. state?
3) What animal has the largest brain?
4) Chinese checkers originated in what country?
5) Is the Northern or Southern Hemisphere warmer?
6) Who holds the NBA career record for most blocks?
7) Who holds the record for most gold medals won in a single Olympics?
8) What does ZIP stand for in ZIP Code?
9) If you wrote out every number in English (one, two, three, etc.), you wouldn't use the letter b until what number?
10) What is the name of Jimmy Stewart's character in the movie *It's a Wonderful Life*?
11) What is Mickey Mouse's dog's name?
12) What long-running television science fiction show first aired in November 1963?
13) On *Star Trek*, what is Captain Kirk's middle name?
14) Who are the only two actors who have won consecutive Best Actor Oscars?
15) What religion was Adolf Hitler?
16) What is the highest elevation city in the world with a population of over 5 million?
17) What is the most malleable naturally occurring metal?
18) What is the second most widely spoken language in the world?
19) What country has the world's largest feral camel herd?
20) What is the longest river in Australia?
21) What television comedy series holds the record for most acting Emmy wins?
22) What instrument did Bob Dylan play in his recording debut?
23) What is arachibutyrophobia?
24) Which U.S. president was a Rhodes Scholar?
25) Where is the Olympic torch originally lit to start its relay to the host site?

Quiz 17 Answers

1) Seven - With a couple of exceptions (sloth and manatee), all mammals, regardless of size or neck, have seven neck vertebrae.

2) Florida – 345 feet between its highest and lowest points

3) Sperm whale – 17 pounds

4) Germany – 1892

5) Northern – 2.7 degrees Fahrenheit warmer due to ocean circulation

6) Hakeem Olajuwon - 3,830

7) Michael Phelps - He won eight gold medals in swimming at the 2008 Beijing games.

8) Zone Improvement Plan

9) One billion

10) George Bailey

11) Pluto

12) *Doctor Who*

13) Tiberius

14) Spencer Tracy – *Captains Courageous* (1937) and *Boys Town* (1938) and Tom Hanks – *Philadelphia* (1993) and *Forrest Gump* (1994)

15) Roman Catholic

16) Bogota, Colombia - 8,596 feet

17) Gold

18) Spanish – Mandarin is first; English is third.

19) Australia – There were as many as 1 million camels at one time; they were imported in the 19th century and many were later set free as the automobile took over. They roam freely with no natural predators.

20) Murray River – 1,558 miles

21) *The Mary Tyler Moore Show* (1970-1977) - 16 wins

22) Harmonica

23) Fear of peanut butter sticking to the roof of your mouth

24) Bill Clinton

25) Temple of Hera in Olympia, Greece

Quiz 18

1) How many U.S. state capitals are named after presidents?
2) Who was Abraham Lincoln's first choice to lead the Union army?
3) What is the end cause of every human death?
4) In the human body, the hallux is more commonly known as what?
5) In Disney's animated *Frozen*, who provides the voice for the central character Anna?
6) What is the second-largest city in England?
7) Scheelite is an important ore of what element?
8) In the movie *Black Panther*, what is the name of the fictional African nation where the action takes place?
9) Several species of what kind of animal can breathe through their anus?
10) Who created television's *Jeopardy!* and *Wheel of Fortune*?
11) What was the first U.S. state to give women the right to vote?
12) For racing purposes, what is the birthday of all horses in the Northern Hemisphere?
13) What sports trophy was successfully defended for the longest time?
14) What is the hardest bone in the human body?
15) What country has the world's highest elevation city?
16) What are the three main types of galaxies?
17) Who is the only Oscar winner whose parents were both Oscar winners?
18) What is the only single by the same artist to go to number one twice?
19) What is the only nation that created nuclear weapons and then voluntarily eliminated them?
20) Adjusted for inflation, what is the highest-grossing comedy movie of all time in the United States?
21) What is the deepest river in South America?
22) The Greek statue *Discobolus* is better known by what name?
23) What is the most commonly occurring place name in the United States?
24) What is the smallest population country with two or more Nobel Prize winners?
25) What country has the southernmost point in Europe?

Quiz 18 Answers

1) Four – Lincoln, Jefferson City, Jackson, Madison
2) Robert E. Lee
3) Cerebral hypoxia – Lack of oxygen to the brain is the final cause of death regardless of what initiates it.
4) Big toe
5) Kristen Bell
6) Birmingham
7) Tungsten
8) Wakanda
9) Turtle - The Fitzroy River turtle, a species that can only be found in the Fitzroy River in Australia, can breathe through its anus; they are constantly pumping water in and out of their anus collecting as much as 70% of all the oxygen they need to survive. Consequently, they can stay underwater for up to three weeks at a time. They are not the only turtle species that can breathe through its anus, but they can use the function to a greater extent.
10) Merv Griffin
11) Wyoming - 1890
12) January 1 – A horse born on December 31 is one year old on January 1.
13) America's Cup for sailing - It was held by the United States for 132 years from its start in 1851 until Australia won in 1983.
14) Jawbone
15) Peru – La Rinconada is a mining town at 16,700 feet in the Andes and has about 30,000 residents.
16) Elliptical, spiral, irregular
17) Liza Minnelli
18) "The Twist" – Chubby Checker in 1960 and 1961
19) South Africa
20) *Home Alone* – 1990
21) Amazon - 328 feet maximum depth
22) *The Discus Thrower*
23) Washington
24) St. Lucia – Caribbean island with 185,000 people and two Nobel Prize winners
25) Greece - Gavdos Island at 34.8 degrees north latitude

Quiz 19

1) Some expensive perfumes still contain poop from what animal?
2) Who has the most all-time number-one hits on Billboard's Hot 100?
3) What horse breed has a greater bone density than other horses, a shorter back with one fewer lumbar vertebrae, and one fewer pair of ribs?
4) The Fahrenheit and Celsius temperature scales are the same at what temperature?
5) Who is the alter ego of the Incredible Hulk?
6) Who was the first African American to win the Best Supporting Actor Oscar?
7) What is the world's highest elevation national capital city?
8) What was George Armstrong Custer's rank when he was killed at Little Bighorn in 1876?
9) What was discovered in 1922 by Howard Carter?
10) How long is an eon?
11) What is the most powerful earthbound explosion ever witnessed by humans?
12) Who is the oldest golfer to win a PGA tour event?
13) Who is the only man to have been both Chief Justice of the U.S. Supreme Court and U.S. president?
14) What two scientists discovered the double-helix structure of DNA in 1953?
15) Who was the first actor or actress to win a competitive acting Oscar for a Walt Disney film?
16) What sport takes place in a 4.55-meter diameter circle?
17) What is the name for a baby opossum?
18) Alexander the Great, Julius Caesar, Genghis Khan, Napoleon, Mussolini, and Hitler all suffered from ailurophobia; what is it?
19) In what state were the only U.S. mainland combat deaths in WWII?
20) What actor was the narrator on Michael Jackson's *Thriller*?
21) Valletta is the capital of what country?
22) What country has the southernmost point in Asia?
23) What U.S. state experienced the world's greatest temperature variation ever recorded in 24 hours?
24) What is the most common birth state for U.S. presidents?
25) Who wrote *The Strange Case of Dr. Jekyll and Mr. Hyde*?

Quiz 19 Answers

1) Sperm whale - Ambergris, a waxy substance produced in the intestines of sperm whales, has been incorporated in perfumes for a long time as a binding agent to help the fragrances linger on the skin and intensify the scent of the perfume.

2) Beatles – 20

3) Arabian

4) 40 degrees below zero

5) Dr. David Banner

6) Louis Gossett Jr. – *An Officer and a Gentleman* (1982)

7) La Paz, Bolivia – 11,942 feet

8) Lieutenant Colonel

9) Tutankhamun's tomb

10) 1 billion years

11) Mount Tambora volcanic eruption in 1815 in Indonesia – The explosion was equivalent to 800 megatons of TNT, 14 times larger than the largest man-made explosion.

12) Sam Snead - 52 years old

13) William Howard Taft

14) James Watson and Francis Crick

15) Julie Andrews – *Mary Poppins* (1964)

16) Sumo wrestling

17) Joey

18) Fear of cats

19) Oregon - On May 5, 1945, a Japanese balloon bomb killed a woman and five children who happened upon it. Balloon bombs had a 33-foot diameter balloon with 35 pounds of explosives and rode the jet stream, making it from Japan to the United States in about three days. An altimeter would trigger a reaction that would jettison the bombs; Japan released about 9,000 of the bombs.

20) Vincent Price

21) Malta

22) Indonesia - Pamana Island at 11 degrees south latitude

23) Montana - On January 23, 1916, Browning, Montana, went from a high of 44 degrees to a low of -56 degrees Fahrenheit in 24 hours.

24) Virginia – eight

25) Robert Louis Stevenson

Quiz 20

1) What country has the southernmost point in mainland North America?

2) Who did the Greeks defeat at the Battle of Marathon in 490 BC?

3) What five surnames have been shared by more than one U.S. president?

4) *All in the Family, The Golden Girls, Will & Grace,* and what other television series are the only ones to win Emmys for all their main cast members?

5) What film series has the most Oscar nominations?

6) What is the only country outside of Europe where Dutch is spoken by most of its population?

7) What is a group of cats called?

8) If a scuba diver suffers from the bends, what gas is being rapidly released from the blood and tissues?

9) Who was the first U.S. president to serve in Congress after his presidency?

10) What is the most populous democratic country?

11) What is the northernmost country in continental South America?

12) What two European countries entered the American Revolutionary War on the side of the Americans?

13) What was the largest denomination currency ever printed in the United States?

14) By area, what is the world's largest sea?

15) Who is the only person to win Oscars for best actress and best song?

16) What was the number-one U.S. box office film released in the 2000s?

17) What psychologist coined the terms introvert and extrovert?

18) What is the second most common element in the universe?

19) Where did Winnie the Pooh live?

20) What private eye hero did Raymond Chandler create?

21) Who wrote "Rhapsody in Blue"?

22) What continent has the highest population density?

23) Who won the 1922 Nobel Prize in Physics for their research on the structure of the atom and the development of the quantum theory?

24) What French philosopher created analytical geometry?

25) What writer established the three laws of robotics?

Quiz 20 Answers

1) Panama - Punta Mariato at 7.2 degrees north latitude
2) Persians - It was during the first Persian invasion of Greece.
3) Adams, Harrison, Johnson, Roosevelt, Bush
4) *Schitt's Creek*
5) *Lord of the Rings* trilogy – 30 nominations
6) Suriname - former Dutch colony in South America
7) Clowder
8) Nitrogen
9) John Quincy Adams
10) India
11) Colombia
12) France and Spain
13) $100,000 bill - It featured a picture of Woodrow Wilson and was only printed for three weeks in December 1934 and January 1935. It was only used for official transactions between Federal Reserve Banks.
14) Philippine – 2.2 million square miles
15) Barbra Streisand
16) *Avatar* – 2009
17) Carl Jung - 1920s
18) Helium - about 25% of the universe by mass
19) Hundred Acre Wood
20) Philip Marlowe
21) George Gershwin
22) Asia
23) Niels Bohr
24) Rene Descartes
25) Isaac Asimov

Quiz 21

1) What is the largest living structure in the world?
2) In *The Terminator*, what is the name of the system that became self-aware and tried to wipe out all humans?
3) What was the first fictional novel blessed by the pope?
4) What is a mononymous person?
5) The feeling of hitting your funny bone is due to hitting what?
6) In 1829, Walter Hunt invented what common fastening item?
7) Which U.S. first lady was later elected to public office?
8) In what country did rock paper scissors originate?
9) What U.S. president wrote 37 books?
10) The hard piece at the end of a shoelace is called what?
11) What country has the most emigrants (people living in other countries)?
12) The five smallest landlocked countries in the world are all on what continent?
13) Who were the first pair of NFL teammates to each rush for 1,000 yards in the same season?
14) Adjusted for inflation, what is the highest-grossing R-rated movie of all time in the United States?
15) Who has appeared on the most *Sports Illustrated* covers?
16) The uppermost region of the sun is called what?
17) What songwriter has the most number-one singles on Billboard's Hot 100?
18) What was the name of the B-29 that dropped the atomic bomb on Hiroshima?
19) What insect may be the most efficient predator and possibly has the best vision of any animal?
20) What was the original flavor of the Twinkie filling?
21) On your body, where would you find your lunula?
22) Oysters can change what about themselves based on environmental conditions?
23) What is the last name of Lucy and Linus from the Peanuts cartoon?
24) What sport originated the term hat trick?
25) What character did Mel Gibson play in *Braveheart*?

Quiz 21 Answers

1) Great Barrier Reef – Situated off the northeastern coast of Australia, it stretches for 1,429 miles and covers an area of approximately 133,000 square miles.

2) Skynet

3) *Ben-Hur: A Tale of the Christ*

4) Someone who is known and addressed by one name

5) Ulnar nerve

6) Safety pin

7) Hilary Clinton

8) China – about 2,000 years ago

9) Theodore Roosevelt

10) Aglet

11) Mexico

12) Europe – Vatican City, San Marino, Liechtenstein, Andorra, Luxembourg

13) Mercury Morris and Larry Csonka – 1972 Miami Dolphins

14) *The Exorcist* – 1973

15) Michael Jordan

16) Corona – It is 1 to 2 million degrees Kelvin.

17) Paul McCartney

18) *Enola Gay*

19) Dragonfly – Humans have three light-sensitive proteins in the eye for red, blue, and green (tri-chromatic vision); dragonflies have up to 33. Their bulbous eyes have 30,000 facets and can see in all directions at once. Studies have also shown that they catch as much as 95% of their intended prey.

20) Banana cream

21) White crescent near the base of your fingernail

22) Gender – It can change back and forth based on conditions.

23) Van Pelt

24) Cricket – The term first appeared in 1858 in cricket when H. H. Stephenson took three wickets with three consecutive balls; fans held a collection for him and presented him with a hat bought with the proceeds.

25) William Wallace

Quiz 22

1) Adjusted for inflation, what is the earliest movie made that has grossed $1 billion in the United States?
2) What European country has no single head of state?
3) What are the only two countries that have won consecutive men's soccer World Cups?
4) Of the 12 men who walked on the moon, 11 were what as children?
5) What movie ends with the line "After all, tomorrow is another day"?
6) If you have a buccula, what do you have?
7) The cheetah is the fastest land animal; what is the second fastest?
8) What film followed the career of athletes Eric Henry Liddell and Harold Abrahams?
9) What major city is on an island in the St. Lawrence River?
10) What is the deepest lake in the United States?
11) What is the name for a male woodchuck?
12) In humans, what is the only muscle not attached on both ends?
13) Who is the author of *Coming of Age in Samoa*, the most widely read book in the field of anthropology?
14) To what bird family does the roadrunner belong?
15) In the movie *Guardians of the Galaxy*, who is Peter Quill's ship named after?
16) What metal currently makes up 92.5% of an Olympic gold medal?
17) What U.S. state has the largest water area?
18) What is the lowest female singing voice called?
19) What is an ungulate?
20) Beethoven's third symphony is nicknamed what?
21) Killer whales aren't whales; what are they?
22) What continent has the most landlocked countries?
23) What was the first toy advertised on U.S. television?
24) Who was the first actor to appear on the cover of *Time* magazine?
25) What is the name of the lion in C.S. Lewis' *The Lion, the Witch and the Wardrobe*?

Quiz 22 Answers

1) *Snow White and the Seven Dwarfs* – 1937
2) Switzerland
3) Italy (1934, 1938) and Brazil (1958, 1962)
4) Boy Scouts
5) *Gone with the Wind* - 1939
6) Double chin
7) Pronghorn antelope – 55 mph
8) *Chariots of Fire* - 1981
9) Montreal, Canada
10) Crater Lake – 1,949 feet
11) He-chuck
12) Tongue
13) Margaret Mead
14) Cuckoo
15) Alyssa Milano – Peter Quill's childhood crush
16) Silver
17) Alaska - 94,743 square miles of water
18) Contralto
19) Hoofed mammal
20) *Eroica*
21) Dolphins – The similarities with dolphins include teeth, streamlined bodies, rounded heads, beak, echolocation, living in pods, and group hunting.
22) Africa – 16
23) Mr. Potato Head – 1952
24) Charlie Chaplin
25) Aslan

Quiz 23

1) What is the easternmost national capital city in Asia?
2) What was the only independent South American country to send troops to fight in WWII?
3) What land animal has the most teeth?
4) What is the most populous country in Central America?
5) What is the barber of Seville's name?
6) Who was the first actor to receive a posthumous Oscar nomination?
7) What is the name for a baby beaver?
8) What is the smallest ocean?
9) What is the only two-sided U.S. state flag (different designs on each side)?
10) What is the densest naturally occurring element?
11) What is the most widely played card game in the world?
12) What animal has the most names?
13) What two U.S. state capitals sit on the borders of other states?
14) On a per-capita basis, what U.S. state produces the most serial killers?
15) What national capital city does the River Liffey flow through?
16) What country has the easternmost point in North America?
17) By area, what is the largest plateau in the world?
18) What television show has the all-time Nielsen season average share rating record?
19) Who is generally given credit for coining the term "rock and roll"?
20) Who holds the NBA record for most career fouls?
21) What is the highest-grossing hand-drawn animated film in history?
22) What is the northernmost city in the world with a population of over 5 million?
23) What country has the most cities with a population of over 1 million?
24) What province or territory has the northernmost point in Canada?
25) What is the most populous country with English as an official language?

Quiz 23 Answers

1) Tokyo, Japan - 139.7 degrees east longitude
2) Brazil
3) Giant armadillo – up to 100
4) Guatemala
5) Figaro
6) James Dean – *East of Eden* in 1956
7) Kit
8) Arctic
9) Oregon
10) Osmium – about 25 times denser than water
11) Solitaire
12) Cougar - It is called puma, mountain lion, panther, catamount, or one of another 40 English, 18 native South American, and 25 native North American names.
13) Carson City, Nevada (California border) and Trenton, New Jersey (Pennsylvania border)
14) Alaska
15) Dublin, Ireland
16) Denmark (Greenland) - Nordostrundingen at 11.5 degrees west longitude
17) Tibetan Plateau - 970,000 square miles in China and Pakistan
18) *I Love Lucy* in 1953 - It had a Nielsen season average share of 67.3, meaning that on average 67.3% of all households viewing television were watching it.
19) Alan Freed
20) Kareem Abdul-Jabbar
21) *The Lion King* - 1994
22) St. Petersburg, Russia - 59.9 degrees north latitude
23) China - over 100 cities
24) Nunavut
25) India

Quiz 24

1) Who was the only U.S. president to win a Pulitzer Prize?
2) What country has the most lakes?
3) What is unique about the word detartrated?
4) How many U.S. presidents were assassinated in office?
5) What is the highest active volcano in the world?
6) What poker hand is known as the dead man's hand?
7) What famous Spanish and English writers both died on April 23, 1616?
8) Who was the first woman appointed to the U.S. Supreme Court?
9) Who plays Gandalf in the movie *The Lord of the Rings: The Return of the King?*
10) Elvis Presley won three Grammy awards; what music category were his three wins?
11) Who created Perry Mason?
12) What is the largest animal ever known to have lived on the earth?
13) What country originated the concentration camp?
14) Who is the only U.S. president ever granted a patent?
15) What are the only three crimes mentioned in the U.S. Constitution?
16) What is the most populous African country?
17) According to the Bible, how long did Methuselah live?
18) What amendment to the U.S. Constitution ended prohibition?
19) What is the longest track and field race in the Olympics?
20) What female mammal can die if she doesn't mate?
21) What is the largest lizard?
22) What epic chronicles events toward the end of the Trojan wars?
23) In the human body, what is otalgia?
24) Who created Tarzan?
25) Based on the speed of the object being hit, what is the fastest racquet sport?

Quiz 24 Answers

1) John F. Kennedy – for Profiles in Courage
2) Canada – It has more lakes than the rest of the world combined.
3) Longest palindrome word in English – same forward and backward
4) Four – Lincoln, Garfield, McKinley, Kennedy
5) Ojos Del Salado – 22,595 feet on the Chile and Argentina border
6) Two black aces and two black eights – This is what Wild Bill Hickok was holding when he was killed.
7) Miguel de Cervantes and William Shakespeare
8) Sandra Day O'Connor – 1981
9) Ian McKellen
10) Gospel – His earliest work was before the Grammys started in 1958.
11) Erle Stanley Gardner
12) Blue whale – up to 100 feet long and 200 tons
13) Great Britain – during the Boer War (1899-1902)
14) Abraham Lincoln - a device that helped buoy vessels over shoals
15) Treason, piracy, counterfeiting
16) Nigeria
17) 969 years
18) 21st
19) 50-kilometer walking race
20) Ferret – The female stays in heat until she mates; if she doesn't, very high levels of estrogen remain in her blood for a long time and can cause aplastic anemia and death. She doesn't have to get pregnant, but she must mate.
21) Komodo dragon – up to 10 feet long and 250 pounds
22) *The Iliad*
23) Earache
24) Edgar Rice Burroughs
25) Badminton – The shuttlecock can travel over 200 mph.

Quiz 25

1) Who is known as the father of modern economics?
2) What is Shakespeare's shortest play?
3) What river goes over Victoria Falls?
4) What human organ has the highest percentage of fat?
5) Who has the most career NBA MVP awards?
6) What two countries have square flags?
7) Under the Articles of Confederation, how many U.S. presidents were there before George Washington?
8) Where in the human body would you find the round window and the oval window?
9) What metal has the highest melting point?
10) What is the only known immortal creature that can transform itself back to a juvenile state?
11) What is the name of Rudolph the Red-Nosed Reindeer's girlfriend?
12) What U.S. state has the largest number of mountains at least 14,000 feet high?
13) Edward Nigma is the birth name of what Batman foe?
14) What is the branch of medicine concerned with disease as it affects a community of people called?
15) What U.S. president imposed the first federal income tax?
16) How many seconds must a cowboy stay aboard a rodeo bronc?
17) British King Edward VIII abdicated his throne to marry who?
18) What metal is the best conductor of electricity?
19) What is a group of rattlesnakes called?
20) Who hit a home run from both sides of the plate in the same game 10 times over their MLB career?
21) What is the only X-rated movie to win the Best Picture Oscar?
22) What television show is generally credited as the inventor of the rerun?
23) What is the only country that borders the Black Sea and the Mediterranean Sea?
24) What is the only Shakespeare play that mentions America?
25) What is the world's best-selling musical instrument?

Quiz 25 Answers

1) Adam Smith
2) *The Comedy of Errors*
3) Zambezi
4) Brain – up to 60% fat
5) Kareem Abdul-Jabbar - six
6) Switzerland and Vatican City
7) Eight - Each served a one-year term.
8) Ear - The round window is an opening from the middle ear to the inner ear; the oval window is an opening that leads from the middle ear to the inner ear.
9) Tungsten – 6,192 degrees Fahrenheit
10) Immortal jellyfish (Turritopsis dohrnii) - Once the adult jellyfish have reproduced, they transform themselves back into their juvenile state. Their tentacles retract, their bodies shrink, and they sink to the ocean floor and start their life cycle all over again. They can do it repeatedly, making them essentially immortal unless they are eaten by another animal or struck by disease.
11) Clarice
12) Colorado - 53
13) Riddler
14) Epidemiology
15) Abraham Lincoln – in 1861 to support the Civil War
16) Eight
17) Wallis Simpson
18) Silver – It is slightly more conductive than copper but much more expensive.
19) A rhumba
20) Mickey Mantle
21) *Midnight Cowboy* (1969) – It was X-rated at the time of the award; in 1971, its rating was changed to R.
22) *I Love Lucy* (1951-1957) - during Lucille Ball's pregnancy
23) Turkey
24) *The Comedy of Errors*
25) Harmonica

Quiz 26

1) What is the largest island on the Australian continent?
2) What real person has been played most often in films?
3) What is the most visited U.S. national park?
4) Among countries that share a land border, what pair of national capital cities are the greatest distance apart?
5) What kind of organism is the world's largest single living organism?
6) What was American folk hero John Chapman's nickname?
7) What is the last word of the Bible?
8) Who invented the electric battery in 1800?
9) Brazil is the largest coffee-producing country; what country is second?
10) Who was the oldest member of the Beatles?
11) What river flows through more countries than any other in the world?
12) In the movie *Ben-Hur*, what is the title character's first name?
13) What sport features a series of bouts known as a barrage?
14) What is the largest 3-digit prime number?
15) A leveret is the young of what animal?
16) Who is the first woman to win comedy acting Emmys for three different roles?
17) Based on the number of weeks at number one on Billboard's Hot 100, who was the top artist of the 2010s?
18) What is the largest desert in Asia?
19) What is the white trail behind a jet plane comprised of?
20) What is the least densely populated European country?
21) Miss Felicity Lemon is what fictional detective's confidential secretary?
22) What Italian artist painted *Birth of Venus*?
23) What country's troops sustained the greatest number of deaths in WWII?
24) What 18th-century writer first penned the line "For fools rush in where angels fear to tread"?
25) What is the largest tree-dwelling animal?

Quiz 26 Answers

1) New Guinea – 303,476 square miles

2) Napoleon Bonaparte

3) Great Smoky Mountains

4) Brasilia, Brazil, and Paris, France (5,427 miles apart) - French Guiana, which borders Brazil, is a part of France, just as Alaska and Hawaii are part of the United States.

5) Mushroom - It is a honey mushroom in Malheur National Forest in Oregon that covers more than three square miles, weighs at least 7,500 tons, and is at least 2,000 years old. DNA testing has confirmed it is the same organism that has spread from a single location thousands of years ago.

6) Johnny Appleseed

7) Amen

8) Alessandro Volta

9) Vietnam

10) Ringo Starr

11) Danube (10 countries) - Germany, Austria, Slovakia, Hungary, Croatia, Serbia and Montenegro, Romania, Bulgaria, Moldova, Ukraine

12) Judah

13) Fencing

14) 997

15) Hare

16) Julia Louis-Dreyfus – *Seinfeld*, *The New Adventures of Old Christine*, *VEEP*

17) Drake

18) Arabian Desert - 900,000 square miles

19) Ice crystals

20) Iceland

21) Hercule Poirot

22) Sandro Botticelli

23) Soviet Union

24) Alexander Pope

25) Orangutan - They are 48-54 inches tall and weigh up to 200 pounds and spend nearly all their time in the forest canopy.

Quiz 27

1) What is the only Middle Eastern country without a desert?
2) Who is the only U.S. president that never lived in Washington, D.C.?
3) What was first published in the *New York World* newspaper on December 21, 1913?
4) What is the name for a group of leopards?
5) What is the only native North American marsupial?
6) How many U.S. presidential candidates have won the popular vote but lost the election?
7) Where does the earth rank in size among the planets in our solar system?
8) What river flows through three U.S. state capitals?
9) What continent has the most freshwater?
10) What animal produces the loudest sound?
11) What country was the first to introduce old-age pensions?
12) What is mainly extracted from pitchblende?
13) What famous artist was struck in the face by a rival and disfigured for life?
14) What is the metal part of a pencil that holds the eraser called?
15) What was the first animated film nominated for the Best Picture Oscar?
16) Unimak is the largest island in what chain?
17) Lateral epicondylitis is the medical name for what common medical condition?
18) What do insects do with their spiracles?
19) What animal has the world's largest egg?
20) The title of whose book translates as *My Struggle*?
21) What is the largest moon in our solar system?
22) What country has the world's oldest working library?
23) Written out in English, what is the second number alphabetically no matter how high you go?
24) In movie making, what job does the gaffer do?
25) What did Simon of Cyrene do in the Bible?

Quiz 27 Answers

1) Lebanon
2) George Washington
3) Crossword puzzle
4) Leap
5) Opossum
6) Four – Andrew Jackson against John Quincy Adams, Samuel Tilden against Rutherford B. Hayes, Al Gore against George W. Bush, and Hilary Clinton against Donald Trump
7) Fifth
8) Missouri River - Bismarck, North Dakota; Pierre, South Dakota; Jefferson City, Missouri
9) Antarctica – The ice sheet contains about 90% of the world's freshwater.
10) Sperm whale – 230 decibels
11) Germany – 1889
12) Uranium
13) Michelangelo
14) Ferrule
15) *Beauty and the Beast* – 1991
16) Aleutian Islands – It is 1,571 square miles.
17) Tennis elbow
18) Breathe
19) Whale shark – The ostrich has the largest laid egg.
20) Adolf Hitler – *Mein Kampf*
21) Ganymede – moon of Jupiter, about 41% of the size of Earth
22) Morocco - The al-Qarawiyyin library in Fez is the world's oldest working library operating since 859 AD.
23) Eight billion
24) Chief electrician
25) Carried Christ's cross

Quiz 28

1) What is the line between two numbers in a fraction called?
2) What do you use your zygomaticus muscle for?
3) What is Carrie's last name in Stephen King's *Carrie*?
4) Who was the original Peeping Tom looking at?
5) Who supposedly ran through the streets naked crying "Eureka!"?
6) Who is the only person to win the Best Actor Oscar three times?
7) Who is the only person to have their own Dewey Decimal classification?
8) What peninsula does Mexico occupy?
9) Who discovered Saturn's rings?
10) What is the name of the fisherman in Ernest Hemingway's *The Old Man and the Sea*?
11) What is the highest mountain in the contiguous 48 U.S. states?
12) What major U.S. city is named after a U.S. vice president of the 1840s?
13) Nudiustertian is a time reference; what does it mean?
14) How many hearts does an octopus have?
15) What country is last alphabetically?
16) Who is the only author to have his works simultaneously number one in television, film, and books?
17) What is the difference between coffins and caskets?
18) Most of the world's supply of cork comes from what type of tree?
19) What metal is the major constituent of rubies?
20) What planet is often called the earth's twin because it is nearly the same size and mass and has similar composition?
21) The atomic mass in the periodic table is stated relative to the weight of what element?
22) Who is the oldest female artist to have a number-one hit on Billboard's Hot 100?
23) What country did the United States buy the Virgin Islands from?
24) Carlo Collodi created what children's character?
25) What U.S. first lady was the first who was not a native speaker of English?

Quiz 28 Answers

1) Vinculum
2) Smiling
3) White
4) Lady Godiva
5) Archimedes
6) Daniel Day-Lewis – *My Left Foot*, *There Will Be Blood*, *Lincoln*
7) William Shakespeare
8) Yucatan
9) Galileo
10) Santiago
11) Mount Whitney, California – 14,505 feet
12) Dallas, Texas – George Mifflin Dallas was vice president for James K. Polk.
13) Day before yesterday
14) Three
15) Zimbabwe
16) Michael Crichton – *ER* (television), *Jurassic Park* (film), *Disclosure* (book)
17) Coffins are typically tapered and six-sided; caskets are rectangular.
18) Oak – cork oak trees predominantly in Portugal and Spain
19) Aluminum
20) Venus
21) Carbon – more specifically carbon-12
22) Cher – age 52 in 1999
23) Denmark
24) Pinocchio
25) Melania Trump

Quiz 29

1) What gives onions their distinctive smell?
2) What U.S. state has the most rainfall?
3) British mathematician Charles Lutwidge Dodgson is better known by what pen name?
4) What is the longest river in the Americas?
5) Of all meteorites ever found, 90% come from what continent?
6) What strait separates Europe and Asia?
7) What was the first James Bond film where M, the head of MI6, is played by a woman?
8) What are the two longest mountain ranges in the United States?
9) Our current North Star is Polaris, it will be replaced by what star in about 13,000 years?
10) What U.S. state's southern border is formed by a river of the same name?
11) What are the three weapons used in fencing?
12) In what book did the utopia Shangri-La appear?
13) What is the only country that has played in every soccer World Cup tournament?
14) Who was the first elected head of a nation to give birth in office?
15) Who was the first actress paid $20 million for a film?
16) What are the first names of the film-making Coen brothers?
17) What year did the last undefeated team win the Super Bowl?
18) What is the least populous country in Europe?
19) What is the shortest complete English sentence?
20) Robert Allen Zimmerman is the real name of what music artist?
21) What country made the world's first feature film in 1906?
22) What is an atom or molecule with a net electric charge due to the loss or gain of one or more electrons called?
23) What is the smallest mammal native to North America?
24) What blood type do mosquitoes like most?
25) Who was the inspiration for the character of Biff Tannen, the bully in the movie *Back to the Future*?

Quiz 29 Answers

1) Sulfur – When cut or crushed, a chemical reaction changes an amino acid to a sulfur compound.
2) Hawaii – 63.7 inches mean annual precipitation
3) Lewis Carroll – *Alice's Adventures in Wonderland*
4) Amazon – 4,345 miles
5) Antarctica
6) Bosporus
7) *GoldenEye* (1995)– Judi Dench
8) Rocky Mountains and Appalachian Mountains
9) Vega - The change is due to a change in the direction the earth's axis points due to a motion called precession. If you think of a spinning top given a slight nudge, the top traces out a cone pattern; that is how the earth moves on its axis. The earth bulges out at the equator, and the gravitational attraction of the moon and sun on the bulge cause the precession that repeats in a 26,000-year cycle that will make Polaris the North Star again in about 26,000 years.
10) Ohio
11) Epee, foil, saber
12) *Lost Horizon*
13) Brazil
14) Benazir Bhutto – Pakistan in 1990
15) Julia Roberts – *Erin Brockovich* (2000)
16) Joel and Ethan
17) 1972 – Miami Dolphins
18) Vatican City
19) Go.
20) Bob Dylan
21) Australia
22) Ion
23) American pygmy shrew - Its body is about two inches long including its tail, and it weighs about 0.07 to 0.16 ounces.
24) Type O
25) Donald Trump

Quiz 30

1) Which U.S. state consumes the most alcohol per capita?
2) What did Alfred Nobel invent to make his money and establish the Nobel Prizes?
3) Writer Eric Blair went by what pen name?
4) What does the J.K. stand for in Harry Potter author J.K. Rowling's name?
5) What is the only South American country that borders the Caribbean Sea and the Pacific Ocean?
6) What is the only insect considered kosher?
7) What novel has the subtitle *The Modern Prometheus*?
8) Who won the most Oscars in a single year?
9) What is the world's highest mountain that isn't part of a range?
10) What species of whale dives deeper and stays underwater the longest?
11) What is the number 10 to the power of 100 called?
12) What television series that started in 1999 won the Outstanding Drama Series Emmy each of its first four seasons?
13) What continent has the lowest highest point?
14) Who was a founder and first director of the New York City Ballet?
15) In music, what is meant by the term pianissimo?
16) What automobile manufacturer invented the three-point seat belt used today?
17) Who is credited with inventing basketball?
18) What is the world's most visited website?
19) What U.S. president was an indentured servant in his early life?
20) Who was Helen Keller's teacher?
21) What country is first alphabetically?
22) What two countries share the longest land border?
23) What was the first U.S. network television show to use the "F" word?
24) What country has the lowest average elevation?
25) What African country was settled by Americans?

Quiz 30 Answers

1) New Hampshire - Its consumption is 103% higher than the national average.
2) Dynamite
3) George Orwell
4) Joanne Kathleen
5) Colombia
6) Locust
7) *Frankenstein*
8) Walt Disney – four in 1953
9) Mount Kilimanjaro – 19,341 feet in Tanzania
10) Sperm whale – They can dive for more than an hour and more than 4,000 feet deep.
11) Googol
12) *The West Wing* (1999–2006)
13) Australia - Mount Kosciuszko at 7,310 feet
14) George Balanchine
15) Very softly
16) Volvo - They gave away the 1962 patent for free to save lives.
17) James Naismith
18) Google
19) Andrew Johnson - He was three years old when his father died, and he and his brother became indentured servants to a tailor.
20) Anne Sullivan
21) Afghanistan
22) United States and Canada – 5,525 miles
23) *Saturday Night Live* - 1981
24) Maldives – 1,200 mostly uninhabited islands in the Indian Ocean; average elevation is 6 feet.
25) Liberia

Quiz 31

1) What is the source of the Mississippi River?
2) What is the second highest elevation national capital city in the world?
3) The United States has the most domestic cats of any country in the world; what country has the second most?
4) Who was the first U.S. president born west of the Mississippi River?
5) What is the oldest U.S. city west of the Rocky Mountains?
6) What is the longest word in the English language with only one vowel?
7) What order of insects contains the most species?
8) What is the oldest city in Canada?
9) How many furlongs are there in a mile?
10) What type of galaxy is the Milky Way?
11) What are the only two mobile national monuments in the United States?
12) Who wrote *The Count of Monte Cristo*?
13) What is the second-highest mountain in North America?
14) The television series *Game of Thrones* is based on a series of novels by what author?
15) Who is the only person to have both a reception and an interception in the Super Bowl?
16) What is the farthest object visible to the naked human eye?
17) What year were women first allowed to compete in the modern Olympics?
18) How many toes does a rhinoceros have on each foot?
19) What is the official language of the United States?
20) What color is a polar bear's skin?
21) Who was the first MLB player to hit 500 home runs and steal 500 bases?
22) What is the national animal of Canada?
23) What is the longest living land mammal after man?
24) Which isotope of carbon is used for radiocarbon dating?
25) Who was the first U.S. president to declare war?

Quiz 31 Answers

1) Lake Itasca, Minnesota
2) Quito, Ecuador - 9,350 feet
3) China
4) Herbert Hoover – Iowa
5) Astoria, Oregon - 1811
6) Strengths – nine letters
7) Beetles
8) St. John's, Newfoundland – founded in 1497
9) Eight
10) Spiral
11) San Francisco's cable cars and the New Orleans Saint Charles streetcar line
12) Alexandre Dumas
13) Mount Logan - 19,551 feet in Yukon province of Canada
14) George R.R. Martin
15) Deion Sanders – He had an interception in Super Bowl XXIX and a reception in Super Bowl XXX.
16) Andromeda Galaxy - It is 2.6 million light-years away and is visible as a dim, large gray cloud almost directly overhead in a clear night sky.
17) 1900
18) Three
19) There isn't one.
20) Black
21) Barry Bonds - 2003
22) Beaver
23) Elephant – up to 86 years
24) Carbon-14
25) James Madison – War of 1812

Quiz 32

1) In the novel *Gulliver's Travels*, what is Gulliver's profession?
2) How many possible ways are there to make change for a dollar?
3) What is the most frequently broken bone in the human body?
4) Who was the original host of television's *Jeopardy!*?
5) What country has the world's longest road tunnel?
6) What is the part of a horse between the fetlock and the hoof called?
7) What were the two cities at the ends of the Pony Express?
8) What U.S. state is closest to Africa?
9) Who is the only U.S. president born on the Fourth of July?
10) Who is known as the father of geometry?
11) What planet in our solar system has the shortest year?
12) What was the first U.S. military academy to admit women?
13) What is the most common team name for U.S. college football teams?
14) What is the smallest landlocked country in the world?
15) What land mammal has the most teeth?
16) What song was originally "Good Morning to All" before the words were changed, and it was published in 1935?
17) How many U.S. presidents were only children?
18) What is the second-largest landlocked country?
19) What is the longest canal in the world?
20) In the Bible, who is Noah's grandfather?
21) What is the lightest known solid element?
22) What country consumes the most meat per capita?
23) What area of London did Jack the Ripper's murders occur in?
24) For animals, what is the summer equivalent to hibernation?
25) What country has the largest number of languages spoken?

Quiz 32 Answers

1) Surgeon
2) 293
3) Clavicle or collar bone
4) Art Fleming – 1964 to 1984
5) Norway – 15.2 miles
6) Pastern
7) St. Joseph, Missouri and Sacramento, California – The Pony Express could transport a letter over 1,800 miles in 10 days but only ran for 18 months, from April 1860 to October 1861.
8) Maine – Quoddy Head peninsula is 3,154 miles from Morocco.
9) Calvin Coolidge
10) Euclid
11) Mercury – 88 Earth days
12) Coast Guard
13) Eagles
14) Vatican City - 0.17 square miles
15) Opossum – 50
16) "Happy Birthday to You"
17) None
18) Mongolia – 604,600 square miles
19) Grand Canal of China – 1,104 miles
20) Methuselah – He fathered Noah's father at age 187.
21) Lithium
22) Australia
23) Whitechapel
24) Estivation – Animals slow their activity for the hot, dry summer months.
25) Papua New Guinea – about 840 languages, one for every 10,000 citizens

Quiz 33

1) Who created Peter Rabbit?

2) Who is likely the bestselling author in history?

3) What are the only three films to win all five major Academy Awards (best picture, director, actor, actress, screenplay)?

4) What is the largest inhabited castle in the world?

5) What scale is used to measure the hardness of minerals?

6) What city has the highest number of American emigrants?

7) About 80% of all plant and animal species found on what very large island are endemic (not found elsewhere)?

8) What crustacean has 10 eyes spread all over their body, including the top of their shell, on their tail, and near their mouth?

9) What is the most populous country the equator passes through?

10) Who was the first U.S. president who went his entire term without a vice president?

11) What city has the largest taxi fleet in the world?

12) What two bodies of water does the Suez Canal connect?

13) If you wanted to dig a hole straight through the center of the earth and end up in China, what country would you have to start in?

14) What is believed to be the oldest continuously inhabited city in South America?

15) What U.S. president often swam in the Potomac River in the buff?

16) What two suits have one-eyed jacks in a deck of cards?

17) What actor has the most Oscar nominations without a win?

18) What actor has been portrayed most on the screen by other actors?

19) In space, what color would the sun appear to be?

20) What species of animal has sub-species including Masai, Reticulated, and Rothschild's?

21) What continent has the largest number of individual deserts?

22) What year was the last man on the moon?

23) Who was the only U.S. president to be held as a prisoner of war?

24) Who holds the NBA career record for most points?

25) What is the only U.S. state that ends with three consonants?

Quiz 33 Answers

1) Beatrix Potter
2) Agatha Christie - 2 to 4 billion copies
3) *It Happened One Night* (1934), *One Flew Over the Cuckoo's Nest* (1975), *The Silence of the Lambs* (1991)
4) Windsor Castle – 590,000 square feet
5) Mohs scale
6) Mexico City
7) Madagascar
8) Horseshoe crab
9) Indonesia
10) John Tyler - He became president on the death of William Henry Harrison and never chose a vice president.
11) Mexico City
12) Red Sea and Mediterranean Sea
13) Argentina
14) Quito, Ecuador - founded in 980 AD
15) John Quincy Adams - He wrote of waking at 4 a.m. and taking a nude morning dip.
16) Hearts and spades – The other suits have two-eyed jacks.
17) Peter O'Toole – eight
18) Charlie Chaplin
19) White
20) Giraffe
21) Asia
22) 1972
23) Andrew Jackson – He joined the Revolutionary War at age 13 and was captured by the British.
24) LeBron James
25) Massachusetts

Quiz 34

1) Humans have about 650 in their entire body; an elephant has 40,000 in its trunk alone; what is it?

2) What is the name of the strong, heavy grating lowered to block the entrance to a castle?

3) What is the technical name for the pouch of a kangaroo or other marsupial?

4) What are the four types of adult human teeth?

5) Who was the only U.S. president whose first language wasn't English?

6) Glass is neither a liquid nor a solid; what is it called?

7) What was the D-Day invasion password?

8) What is the more common name for an animal's vibrissae?

9) What is the largest venomous snake?

10) How many compartments does a cow's stomach have?

11) Who said, "Tis better to have loved and lost than never to have loved at all"?

12) In what country were the Guns of Navarone installed?

13) What was the first NBA team to win 10 championships?

14) What is the fastest spinning planet in our solar system?

15) What U.S. state capital was once the national capital?

16) What does a polyandric woman have more than one of?

17) What country has the Great Victoria Desert?

18) What is the most money you can have in change and not be able to make change for a dollar?

19) Who wrote the music *Ride of the Valkyries*?

20) What classic U.S. sitcom was based on the British show *Till Death Us Do Part*?

21) What artist had the first record to sell over 1 million copies?

22) Who was the first Major League Baseball pitcher to strike out 4,000 batters?

23) What was the first U.S. primetime animated television series?

24) What is the only country to win a gold medal at every Summer Olympics?

25) Since Joe DiMaggio's record, who has the longest MLB consecutive game streak with at least one hit?

Quiz 34 Answers

1) Muscles
2) Portcullis
3) Marsupium
4) Incisors, canines, premolars, molars
5) Martin Van Buren - He spoke Dutch as his first language and learned English in school.
6) Amorphous solid - a state somewhere between liquid and solid
7) Mickey Mouse
8) Whiskers
9) King cobra
10) Four
11) Alfred Lord Tennyson
12) Turkey
13) Boston Celtics - 10th championship in 1967-68 season
14) Jupiter - 28,273 mph at the equator compared to 1,038 mph for the Earth
15) Annapolis, Maryland
16) Husband
17) Australia - 220,000 square miles
18) $1.19 - three quarters, four dimes, and four pennies
19) Richard Wagner
20) *All in the Family*
21) Enrico Caruso – 1902
22) Nolan Ryan
23) *The Flintstones* – 1960
24) Great Britain - Due to boycotts, only Great Britain, France, Australia, Greece, and Switzerland have participated in every Summer Olympics.
25) Pete Rose - 44 in 1978

Quiz 35

1) What are the four railways in the game Monopoly?
2) What country has the longest coastline?
3) What is the study of movement in relation to human anatomy called?
4) What is the most commonly used noun in English?
5) What country is closest to 0 degrees latitude and 0 degrees longitude (the intersection of the equator and the prime meridian)?
6) If you suffer from epistaxis, what is wrong?
7) What animal has the densest fur?
8) What two actresses share the record with five consecutive Best Actress Oscar nominations?
9) What was the first nation to have a female prime minister?
10) What U.S. landmark became 1,313 feet shorter in 1980?
11) What poet won the Pulitzer Prize four times?
12) The word salary derives from the Latin "salarium" that referred to a soldier's allowance to buy what?
13) By area, what is the largest country in Central America?
14) What U.S. founding father was carried to the Constitutional Convention in a sedan chair carried by prisoners?
15) The character of the boy Dill Harris who is visiting for the summer in *To Kill a Mockingbird* is based on what famous person?
16) What country has the world's highest unclimbed mountain?
17) What standard international unit for measuring area is equal to 2.471 acres?
18) Inspired by burrs, George de Mestral invented what product in the 1940s?
19) What U.S. state has a Union Jack on its flag?
20) What novel is set in a desert with giant sandworms?
21) What is a monotreme?
22) Who was the first unseeded man to win Wimbledon?
23) What real-life person is Captain Morgan rum named after?
24) What is the largest volume lake in North America?
25) What city was the first U.S. national capital?

Quiz 35 Answers

1) Reading, Pennsylvania, B&O, Short Line
2) Canada
3) Kinesiology
4) Time
5) Ghana - The equator and prime meridian intersect 380 miles south of Ghana in the Gulf of Guinea.
6) Nosebleed
7) Sea otter - They have up to 1 million hairs per square inch on the densest parts of their bodies.
8) Bette Davis (1938-1942) and Greer Garson (1941-1945)
9) Sri Lanka – 1960
10) Mount St. Helens
11) Robert Frost
12) Salt - In ancient Rome, soldiers were sometimes paid in salt or given an allowance to purchase it.
13) Nicaragua – 50,338 square miles
14) Benjamin Franklin
15) Truman Capote – He was a childhood friend and neighbor of author Harper Lee, and they remained lifelong friends.
16) Bhutan - Gangkhar Puensum at 24,840 feet is the tallest unclimbed mountain in the world. It has been off-limits to climbers since 1994 when Bhutan prohibited all mountaineering above 6,000 meters due to spiritual and religious beliefs.
17) Hectare – It is equal to the area of a square with 100-meter sides (10,000 square meters).
18) Velcro
19) Hawaii
20) *Dune*
21) Egg-laying mammal
22) Boris Becker - 1985
23) Sir Henry Morgan - He was a 17th-century Welsh privateer. A privateer is essentially a pirate who is sanctioned by the government; he was hired by the British to protect their interests in the Caribbean from the Spanish.
24) Lake Superior - United States and Canada
25) Philadelphia, Pennsylvania

Quiz 36

1) Under the Articles of Confederation, how many U.S. presidents were there before George Washington?
2) In Greek mythology, who ferries the dead across the river Styx?
3) What Italian tractor maker first tried making cars in the 1960s?
4) Who is the youngest ever U.S. president?
5) What four seas are named for colors?
6) What animal has the longest tongue relative to its size?
7) Who developed the first antibiotic, penicillin?
8) Who was the first African American to win a Wimbledon singles title?
9) What country has the easternmost point in mainland South America?
10) What was the first team sport added to the Olympics?
11) Who was the first U.S. vice president to become president after the death of the president?
12) What is the first city to host the Summer Olympics three times?
13) What two South American countries share the region of Patagonia?
14) If something is quotidian, how often does it occur?
15) What nationality was Cleopatra?
16) What is the most-visited paid monument in the world?
17) How many legs do butterflies have?
18) What U.S. city was first to host the Olympics?
19) What European country has the highest population density?
20) What actor or actress has the longest time between their first and last Oscars?
21) In Greek mythology, whose son flew too close to the sun on waxen wings?
22) What scale is used to measure wind speed?
23) How many countries are in Central America?
24) What were the last four states to join the United States?
25) What is the only country to have won medals in the Winter Olympics but never in the Summer Olympics?

Quiz 36 Answers

1) Eight - Each served a one-year term.
2) Charon
3) Ferruccio Lamborghini
4) Theodore Roosevelt – 42
5) Red, Black, Yellow, White
6) Chameleon
7) Alexander Fleming - 1928
8) Althea Gibson - 1957
9) Brazil - Ponta do Seixas at 34.8 degrees west longitude
10) Soccer - 1900
11) John Tyler – He became president in 1841 after the death of William Henry Harrison.
12) London – 1908, 1948, 2012
13) Chile and Argentina
14) Daily
15) Greek
16) Eiffel Tower
17) Six
18) St. Louis – 1904
19) Monaco – over 47,000 per square mile
20) Katharine Hepburn – 48 years from 1933 to 1981
21) Daedalus
22) Beaufort
23) Seven - Belize, Costa Rica, El Salvador, Guatemala, Honduras, Nicaragua, Panama
24) New Mexico, Arizona, Alaska, Hawaii
25) Liechtenstein

Quiz 37

1) Who was the first person other than royalty to appear on a British stamp?
2) Hawaiian pizza was invented in what country?
3) What does WIFI stand for?
4) What U.S. state has the highest average elevation?
5) The United States lost the men's basketball gold medal for the first time at what Olympics?
6) What is the oldest English-speaking university in the world?
7) In what method of singing does the singer alternate between natural voice and falsetto?
8) What African national capital city is named for a U.S. president?
9) Who was the first Roman Catholic U.S. vice president?
10) What literary character was the Thane of Cawdor?
11) What U.S. president was the youngest naval aviator in U.S. history at the age of 18?
12) Who was the first athlete to win the same Olympic running event three times?
13) How many eyes are there in a deck of 52 cards?
14) What is the oldest alcoholic beverage to gain widespread popularity?
15) What Shakespeare play contains the line "Something is rotten in the state of Denmark"?
16) Who was the first U.S. president term-limited by the 22nd Amendment?
17) What makes an animal viviparous?
18) Who was the first African American in space?
19) What does ambisinistrous mean?
20) What country contains the geographic center of South America?
21) Who wrote the *Jungle Book* series?
22) What periodic table element has the shortest name?
23) Domestic cats don't seem to have an overall paw preference for right or left like humans do, but they do have a gender-based preference; what paw do male cats favor?
24) Adjusted for inflation, what is the highest-grossing western film of all time in the United States?
25) Who reached the South Pole in January 1912 only to find that Amundsen had gotten there first?

Quiz 37 Answers

1) William Shakespeare

2) Canada - It was first created in 1962 in Ontario, Canada.

3) Nothing – It doesn't mean wireless fidelity or anything else; it is just a branding name picked by a company hired for the purpose.

4) Colorado – 6,800 feet average

5) 1972 Munich

6) Oxford - It existed about 350 years before the start of the Inca and Aztec empires. There was teaching at Oxford as early as 1096, making it the third-oldest university in continuous operation in the world and the oldest English-speaking university.

7) Yodeling

8) Monrovia, Liberia

9) Joseph Biden

10) Macbeth

11) George H.W. Bush

12) Usain Bolt - 100 and 200-meter races in 2008, 2012, 2016

13) 42 – The jack of hearts, jack of spades, and the king of diamonds are in profile with only one eye showing.

14) Mead – about 2000 BC from fermenting honey

15) *Hamlet*

16) Dwight D. Eisenhower

17) Viviparous animals are born as live young individuals; they do not lay eggs.

18) Guion Bluford - 1983

19) No good with either hand - opposite of ambidextrous

20) Paraguay

21) Rudyard Kipling

22) Tin

23) Left - Females are significantly more likely to be right paw dominant.

24) *Butch Cassidy and the Sundance Kid* – 1969

25) Captain Robert Scott

Quiz 38

1) What country has the world's second-largest Christian population?
2) Professional bowler Walter Ray Williams Jr. is also a nine-time world champion in what other sport?
3) How many species of bear are alive today?
4) What was the first lighthouse?
5) Who would use a plessor?
6) What is the only borough of New York City that is not mainly on an island?
7) What is the most populous island in the Mediterranean Sea?
8) Good King Wenceslas was king of what country?
9) Who was the first gymnast to score a perfect 10 in the Olympics?
10) Which of the Great Lakes doesn't share a border with Canada?
11) What is Europe's largest island?
12) Who was the first U.S. president to have been divorced?
13) Who was the second man on the moon?
14) What country has the most beaches?
15) In what country or territory is the northernmost active volcano in the world?
16) What century is the setting for the original *Star Trek* television series?
17) What novel ends with "It is a far better thing I do, than I have ever done; it is a far, far better rest that I go to than I have ever known"?
18) What country did the United States defeat in the men's hockey gold medal game in the 1980 Lake Placid Olympics?
19) In the 2001 film *Ocean's Eleven*, who plays the role originated by Frank Sinatra in the 1960 original?
20) What does the Spanish snack or appetizer tapas literally mean?
21) According to the Old Testament, who planted the first vineyard?
22) What Polish astronomer demonstrated in 1512 that the sun is the center of the solar system?
23) What fish's name is thought to derive from the Latin meaning "to leap"?
24) How many times does the moon revolve around the earth in a year?
25) What was Al Capone finally imprisoned for in 1931?

Quiz 38 Answers

1) Brazil

2) Horseshoes

3) Eight – sun, sloth, spectacled, American black, Asian black, brown, polar, giant panda

4) Pharos of Alexandria – 280 BC

5) Doctor – It is the small hammer with a rubber head used to test reflexes.

6) Bronx

7) Sicily

8) Bohemia - current Czech Republic

9) Nadia Comaneci - 1976

10) Lake Michigan

11) Great Britain - 80,823 square miles

12) Ronald Reagan

13) Buzz Aldrin

14) Australia - Its coastline is over 16,000 miles long and has over 10,000 beaches.

15) Norway - Beerenberg volcano on the Norwegian island of Jan Mayen in the Arctic Ocean at 71.1 degrees north latitude

16) 23rd century

17) *A Tale of Two Cities*

18) Finland - They defeated the Soviet Union 4-3 in the semi-final "Miracle on Ice" game.

19) George Clooney – plays Danny Ocean

20) Covers or lids

21) Noah

22) Nicholas Copernicus

23) Salmon

24) 13

25) Income tax evasion

Quiz 39

1) What are the four major human blood types?

2) What political cartoonist popularized the use of the elephant and donkey as symbols of the two main U.S. political parties?

3) How many sides does the Great Pyramid of Giza have?

4) John Montagu is credited with inventing what food item?

5) What is the highest mountain outside of Asia?

6) Most members of the nightshade family that includes tomatoes, potatoes, eggplants, and green peppers contain small quantities of what stimulant?

7) What was the last animated film personally supervised by Walt Disney?

8) Who was the first MLB player with 3,000 hits and 500 home runs in their career?

9) What is the specific name for a female pig less than six months old?

10) What country originated the story of Cinderella?

11) What medical condition is detected using the Ishihara test?

12) What country created the Smurfs?

13) Jesus' name translated directly from Hebrew to English would be what?

14) What gas makes up most of the earth's atmosphere?

15) What three actors played *The Good, The Bad, and The Ugly*?

16) What element, previously used in the production of felt, led to the expression "mad as a hatter"?

17) Measured from base to summit, what is the tallest mountain in the world?

18) How many letters are in the shortest country name in the world?

19) What is the only dog breed specifically mentioned in the Bible?

20) What name is given to a ring-shaped coral reef?

21) Who won the first U.S. presidential election after the 26th amendment gave 18-year-olds the right to vote?

22) What country has the longest coastline in South America?

23) What country was known to Europeans as Cathay from the 11th to the 16th century?

24) What is the only South American country with English as an official language?

25) Brass is an alloy of what two metals?

Quiz 39 Answers

1) A, B, AB, O
2) Thomas Nast
3) Eight – Each of the four sides are split from base to tip by slight concave indentations.
4) Sandwich – fourth Earl of Sandwich
5) Aconcagua – 22,841 feet in Argentina
6) Nicotine
7) *The Jungle Book* – 1967
8) Willie Mays – 1970
9) Gilt
10) China
11) Color blindness
12) Belgium
13) Joshua – Jesus comes from translating Hebrew to Greek to Latin to English.
14) Nitrogen – about 78%
15) Clint Eastwood, Lee Van Cleef, Eli Wallach
16) Mercury – It caused poisoning.
17) Mauna Kea in Hawaii – Measured from the seafloor where it starts, Mauna Kea is about 33,500 feet tall, almost 4,500 feet taller than Mount Everest; it only reaches 13,796 feet above sea level.
18) Four letters – Chad, Togo, Mali, Iraq, Iran, Oman, Laos, Niue, Fiji, Cuba, Peru
19) Greyhound
20) Atoll
21) Richard Nixon
22) Brazil – 4,934 miles
23) China
24) Guyana
25) Copper and zinc

Quiz 40

1) Who was the first person to win a gold medal in three different Olympics?

2) Who was the only main cast member to be in both the movie and television versions of M*A*S*H?

3) What U.S. television show has aired the most episodes?

4) What country and its territories cover the most time zones?

5) Who is the only person named Associated Press athlete of the year in two different sports?

6) In astronomy, who coined the term "Big Bang"?

7) How many vertebrae are in the human spine?

8) What type of creature lives in a sett?

9) What country spans the Pacific Ocean, the Caribbean Sea, the Amazon River, and the Andes Mountains?

10) Measured by its share of the world's population, what is the largest empire in history?

11) What insect lives the longest?

12) What U.S. president was once a fashion model?

13) Who are the only two artists to win best new artist and record, album, and song of the year Grammys in the same year?

14) What year did the first NFL indoor game take place?

15) What province or territory has the southernmost point in Canada?

16) The poodle dog breed didn't originate in France; where did it originate?

17) Who is the only person to win *Time* magazine's person of the year three times?

18) Galvanizing is the process of applying a protective coating of what metal to steel or iron to prevent rusting?

19) What are camel hair brushes typically made from?

20) What is the only major nut tree indigenous to North America?

21) What is the largest island in Canada?

22) What is the deepest river in the world?

23) What are the only two sequels to win Best Picture Oscars?

24) What is the most populous city in Canada?

25) Through what town did Lady Godiva ride naked?

Quiz 40 Answers

1) Sonja Henie – figure skating in 1928, 1932, 1936
2) Gary Burghoff – Radar O'Reilly
3) *SportsCenter* – over 50,000 unique episodes since 1979
4) France with 12 time zones – The United States and Russia each cover 11 time zones.
5) Babe Didrikson Zaharias – track and field in 1932; golf in 1945, 1946, 1947, 1950, 1954
6) Fred Hoyle – He was an English astronomer and coined it in 1949 on a BBC radio broadcast.
7) 33
8) Badger
9) Colombia
10) Persian Empire – It accounted for approximately 44% of the world's population in 480 BC. In contrast, the British Empire accounted for about 23% of the world's population at its peak.
11) Termite queen – They have been known to live for at least 50 years, and some scientists believe they may live to 100.
12) Gerald Ford – *Cosmopolitan* and *Look* magazines in the 1940s
13) Christopher Cross (1981) and Billie Eilish (2020)
14) 1932 – With temperatures of 30 below in Chicago, the Bears played a game indoors against the Portsmouth Spartans in the Chicago Stadium, which was used mainly for horse shows; they played on a modified 80-yard field.
15) Ontario
16) Germany – It comes from the German "pudel," which means "to splash about."
17) Franklin D. Roosevelt
18) Zinc
19) Squirrel hair
20) Pecan – They have not been found growing naturally anywhere else in the world.
21) Baffin – 195,928 square miles
22) Congo – up to 750 feet deep
23) *The Godfather Part II* and *The Lord of the Rings: The Return of the King*
24) Toronto
25) Coventry, England

Anything and Everything

If you enjoyed this book and learned a little and would like others to enjoy it also, please put out a review or rating. If you scan the QR code below, it will take you directly to the Amazon review and rating page.